Why Did You Die?

Activities to Help Children Cope with Grief & Loss

ERIKA LEEUWENBURGH, LPC
ELLEN GOLDRING, LPC

Instant Help Books
A Division of New Harbinger Publications, Inc.

Publisher's Note

This publication is designed to provide accurate and authoritative information in regard to the subject matter covered. It is sold with the understanding that the publisher is not engaged in rendering psychological, financial, legal, or other professional services. If expert assistance or counseling is needed, the services of a competent professional should be sought.

Distributed in Canada by Raincoast Books

Copyright © 2008 by Erika Leeuwenburgh and Ellen Goldring
        Instant Help Books
        A Division of New Harbinger Publications, Inc.
        5674 Shattuck Avenue
        Oakland, CA 94609
        www.newharbinger.com

Cover design by Amy Shoup
Illustrations by Julie Olson

Library of Congress Cataloging-in-Publication Data

Leeuwenburgh, Erica.
  Why did you die? : activities to help children cope with grief and loss / Erica Leeuwenburgh and Ellen Goldring.
    p. cm.
  ISBN-13: 978-1-57224-604-1 (pbk. : alk. paper)
  ISBN-10: 1-57224-604-9 (pbk. : alk. paper)
  1. Grief in children. 2. Loss (Psychology) in children. 3. Children and death. 4. Bereavement in children. I. Goldring, Ellen B. (Ellen Borish), 1957- II. Title.
  BF723.G75L44 2008
  155.9'37083--dc22

                  2008002069

10   09   08

10 9 8 7 6 5 4 3 2 1

To Zachary, Alexandra, Marly, and Lyla
and the children who have shared
their life and death experiences with us

Contents

To Parents   vii

Grief and Developmental Stages   ix

How Children Grieve   xiii

Complicated and Traumatic Grief   xv

Dear Kids   xvi

Activity 1: Everything Changes   1

Activity 2: Changes You Can Control and Changes You Can't   4

Activity 3: How You See Yourself and How Others See You   7

Activity 4: You Have Many Feelings   9

Activity 5: Your Life Is a Journey   12

Activity 6: You Have a Support System   15

Activity 7: Every Family Is Unique   18

Activity 8: A Special Place Can Feel Good   21

Activity 9: A Gift from Your Loved One   24

Activity 10: Everything Has a Life Span   27

Activity 11: There Are Many Causes of Death   29

Activity 12: How Your Loved One Died   31

Activity 13: Special Things You Did with Your Loved One   34

Activity 14: What Your Loved One Enjoyed   36

Activity 15: The Idea of Death Looks Different to Each of Us   39

Activity 16: Illnesses, Accidents, and Natural Events   41

Activity 17: Death Stops the Body from Working   44

Activity 18: This Death Was Not Your Fault   46

Activity 19: The Funeral Service   48

Activity 20: People Give Gifts to Show They Care   51

Activity 21: A Place People Go to Remember   54

Activity 22: Beliefs About What Happens After Death   57

Activity 23: Keeping a Feeling of Togetherness   60

Activity 24: Feelings of Grief Can Change   **63**

Activity 25: People Grieve Differently   **66**

Activity 26: Wishing Things Could Be Different   **69**

Activity 27: Times You Think About Your Loved One   **71**

Activity 28: Pretending to Be a Superhero   **75**

Activity 29: It's Okay to Play   **78**

Activity 30: Sharing Your Worries   **81**

Activity 31: When You Feel Angry   **84**

Activity 32: Some Things Change and Some Remain the Same   **87**

Activity 33: You Will Always Be You   **90**

Activity 34: Taking Something to the Place You Remember Your Loved One   **93**

Activity 35: Things You Wish You Had Said   **96**

Activity 36: Honoring the Memory of Your Loved One   **99**

Activity 37: Memories Are Important   **102**

Activity 38: Sharing Memories with Others   **105**

Activity 39: Life Has Ups and Downs   **108**

Activity 40: Taking Care of Yourself   **111**

To Parents

Although we like to think of childhood as a time of playful innocence, tens of thousands of children experience the loss of a loved one before the age of twelve. Most commonly it is a grandparent who dies, but sometimes it is an aunt or uncle, a parent, or even a sibling.

Death is hard for grown-ups to accept and understand, and with fewer emotional resources and less life experience, children may have a particularly hard time. This book can help.

Begin by reading the simple and straightforward explanations of how children experience grief at different ages. You will find thoughtful recommendations to help children at every stage between two and twelve.

Then look through the activities and select the ones that seem most appropriate for the child you are concerned about. Not every activity will apply to every child. Some of the most important things children will learn are:

- There are some things you can control in your life and some you can't (Activity 2).
- Every living thing has a life span (Activity 10).
- People have different ideas about death (Activities 13 and 22).
- People grieve differently (Activity 26).
- It's okay to be happy, even though you are grieving (Activity 29).
- Memories of our loved ones are important and they should be shared (Activities 37 and 38).

This workbook provides an entirely new way for you to help a child grieve. The activities in this workbook will not only help children through their time of loss, but will also teach them ways to cope with all of life's stresses.

As you help a child with his grieving process, you will probably find out that it is difficult for him to talk about certain issues. Never force a child to talk if he doesn't want to. The best way to get children to open up is to be a good role model. Talk about your thoughts, feelings, and experiences as they relate to each activity, stressing the positive ways that you cope with problems. Even if the child doesn't say a thing back, your words will have an important impact.

This workbook was designed to help any child who has had a significant loss, but some children may need some additional help as well. Some children experience a significant depression triggered by a loss, even when it is not a close family member. Other children begin having nightmares, specific fears, or general anxiety. If you are at all concerned about your child's reaction to loss, you should certainly consider consulting a trained counselor. Besides individual counseling, your child many benefit by talking to other children who are going through a grieving process. Most hospitals, schools, and community mental health centers can help you find groups in your area to help children deal with loss.

If the person who died was close to you, you might also consider grief counseling for yourself. It is a very valuable experience that will go a long way toward helping you give support to the child you are concerned about.

There is no wrong way to use this workbook to help your child as long as you remain patient and respectful of a child's feelings.

Sincerely,

Lawrence E. Shapiro, Ph.D.

Grief and Developmental Stages

How children experience grief changes with their developmental stages. Although individual children vary, there are characteristics typical of each stage. This section describes those characteristics and offers recommendations to help children cope.

Under Age Two

Children in this age group readily identify with their parents, siblings, and caretakers, and have established relationships with them. While they are profoundly aware of change, they do not have the sophisticated verbal skills to express their thoughts and feelings. Instead, their behavior will demonstrate the distress they are experiencing. Given a loving and nurturing environment, infants and toddlers can adapt and adjust to the death of a loved one.

Recommendations

Using basic language, verbalize that the loved one has died and will not come back. Events related to the death can be described in simple terms as well. It is extremely important to maintain children's regular routines as closely as possible. Keep their familiar items nearby and try to minimize change in their environment. Children who have lost their primary caretakers may find it soothing to have a shirt or pillow that holds the scent of their loved one. A photo book that illustrates the child with the deceased can reinforce positive memories and comfort the child.

From Three to Five Years Old

At this stage, children have not yet developed abstract thinking. They do not understand that death is permanent and may often ask when their loved one will come back. These questions are usually more unnerving for adults; children are simply trying to master a concept that is even difficult for adults to understand. Because children think literally, words intended to protect them can lead to misunderstanding and fears. For example, a child who is told that death is like sleeping may begin to fear going to bed at night. Children at this age also do not comprehend that events around them occur without their involvement. This egocentric way of thinking is a normal part of their development. It can lead some children to feel responsible for the death of their loved one, even to the point of "magical thinking," in which children believe their thoughts can cause events. Believing that the death is connected to them rather than something outside their control, they may also feel rejected and abandoned.

Recommendations

Three- to five-year-olds need opportunities to play, ask questions, and share memories in order to thrive. It is helpful to be honest, use simple language, and take time to talk. The best way to describe death is by stating that the person's body has stopped working, rather than using euphemisms such as "sleeping" or "gone away." To prevent confusion that can lead to anxiety, others involved in the child's life should try to use consistent language. Children must be reassured that the death is not their fault and their loved one did not want to leave them. This age group can benefit tremendously from having a choice about participating in the funeral arrangements.

From Six to Nine Years Old

This age group begins to understand that death is permanent and that the person will not return. They may have a concept of heaven or some kind of lasting separation and begin to comprehend death more realistically, but this tends to be limited to the elderly and disabled. Six- to nine-year-olds can conceptualize death as a character who takes someone away rather than an event that impacts everyone. They are likely to be very concerned about their own safety and well-being, possibly asking about who will take care of them. Their thinking is still concrete, which may cause them to ask questions about death. While these questions may revolve around the physical body and seem inappropriate to adults, the information they seek will help them feel safer and more in control. Early attention to the depth of their grief will help these children heal from wounds created by profound loss.

Recommendations

It is helpful to encourage and answer questions in a clear, honest, and straightforward manner, giving the message that painful issues can be discussed and shared. Six- to nine-year-olds can understand the body's functions and process a more detailed explanation about death and its causes. By normalizing death, responses to questions, such as why the body is cold, may reduce anxiety. It is important to give these children choices about attending the funeral service or going to the cemetery.

From Ten to Twelve Years Old

As their abstract thinking develops, children in this age group begin to have a more sophisticated understanding of death. They know that death is universal and that they too will die someday. They often ask about how the person died and what happens to the body, and they may have a need for seemingly graphic descriptions. Again, these questions may be unnerving for adults and perceived as inappropriate, but they simply reflect the developmental need to master the concepts of death and dying. In this age range, there is a developing sense of moral awareness, which can lead to the perception that death is a punishment. Children's ability to express their thoughts and feelings can help adults explore and demystify their perceptions about death. Ten- to twelve-year-olds are also mature enough to be interested in planning the funeral and possibly speaking during services.

Recommendations

The need of this age group is to understand that children cannot prevent death and that no one is being punished. It helps to simply state that sometimes things happen for which there are no answers and to model the ability to discuss and share authentic feelings of grief. Understanding that adults are affected by grief creates a shared experience that strengthens family relationships. However, while it is all right for adults to express their feelings and show the impact of the loss, it is important that they not overwhelm children with their grief.

From Thirteen to Eighteen Years Old

Most adolescents have a full understanding of death. They begin to integrate a spiritual approach and can conceptualize the abstract components of death and dying. Developmentally, adolescents are experiencing a sense of their own immortality, often taking risks, romanticizing death, and exploring their own limits and boundaries. The reality of death can be overwhelming, shattering their idealized and safe world. It is not unusual for this age group to deny the impact of death and avoid direct conversation about the death of their loved one. Nevertheless, it is helpful to share feelings and memories and give choices about involvement in funeral arrangements, remaining aware that adolescents may choose not to engage. Adolescence is a period of growing independence when teens develop their identities. By encouraging expression of feelings without forcing, pushing, or creating expectations, adults can foster comfort, mutual respect, and understanding.

Recommendations

Some of the best conversations happen at unexpected times—riding in the car, getting ready for school, and other informal moments. In this type of relaxed communication, the contact can be brief and meaningful but not pressured, so adolescents feel less confronted. We highly recommend that adolescents be involved in memorializing their loved ones through creative expression and participation in family events or rituals.

How Children Grieve

Grief is not limited to the period when death occurs. Grieving children and adolescents experience their loss over the course of their lives, and the activities in this book can be used at different developmental phases.

As they pass through each developmental stage, children gain greater understanding and grieve their loss in a new way. Life's milestones also can bring grief back to the surface: a boy whose mother died when he was six may grieve her loss again when he graduates from high school.

There are many outdated beliefs about what is helpful for children trying to cope with death, for example, that left to their own devices, children will get over a loss or that not giving children much information about death is a way to protect them. Fallacies like these can be damaging. Adults need to be aware of how children experience their grief and must encourage dialogue that allows children to express their feelings. Children benefit from age-appropriate information and open communication.

Children are different from adults. This simple fact is imperative for adults to remember when observing a grieving child. The child's behavior should not be interpreted with an adult's frame of reference. A child can play with family or friends at the funeral and still be in the midst of grieving.

Children grieve in short spurts and differently than adults, although just as powerfully. They are action oriented and express their feelings through day-to-day activities. They tolerate communicating grief for short periods of time and then move to familiar activities or experiences. It is normal for a child to cry about the loss for a few minutes and then ask to go to the park, play with friends, or ride a bike.

Children who are grieving often regress, engaging in behaviors and activities from an earlier developmental stage. This process is emotionally necessary for children who are overwhelmed by the uncertainties and changes that accompany death. It is not unusual for grieving children who have slept alone to want to return to their parents' bed or for children who had given up thumb sucking to begin again. They may have tantrums or emotional outbursts that show a lack of control. It is important that adults not become punitive at this transitional time and comfort children instead. Acknowledging their feelings of grief and talking about the changes they have experienced can help.

Children may experience separation anxiety after the death of a loved one. They may not want to go to school and may want to be with their parents more frequently. It is normal for them to become concerned that other people might die as well; worrying about the welfare of their caretakers becomes paramount. It helps to clarify the circumstances of the death and describe the safety of remaining family members. Reiterating that everyone will be fine and describing separations and reunions in advance can help meet their great need for reassurance.

Seemingly small losses—a missing toy, an unfulfilled expectation, or simply not being able to have a third cookie—may trigger strong emotions that are actually related to the primary loss. These reactions offer the opportunity to help children by talking about what is most upsetting—the death of their loved one. Projecting how they are feeling about the death, they may describe their completion of the activities in this book as "messed up," "not good enough," or "bad." Simply supporting their efforts and reflecting that it sometimes feels like nothing works out right can help.

Group support with other children who have similar experiences can be beneficial by decreasing children's sense of isolation and increasing their ability to understand and cope with grief. This workbook can be used with an individual child or in a group setting; children may feel more at ease with peers who are exploring the same issues and working on the same activities.

Parents and children grieving at the same time pose many challenges that can be alleviated by patience and compassion. These guidelines focus on children's grief and how adults can help, but the desire to nurture, heal, and comfort children can be compromised for adults who are in the midst of their own grief. Support resources, such as school counselors, spiritual counselors, peer support groups, relatives, and friends, can offer special time to children and information or help to adults. This book offers creative experiences for a child and an adult to share. The adult is welcome to participate or simply to witness and reflect the child's process.

Complicated and Traumatic Grief

Complicated grief involves many prior issues, such as other deaths or losses, emotional vulnerability, or multiple deaths at one time. Traumatic grief results from sudden, unexpected, violent, or catastrophic deaths. The following behaviors are signs for concern when displayed over a period of more than one month after the death. They suggest the need for professional advice and bereavement counseling.

Shift in Sleep Patterns

Children may be unable to fall asleep, wake throughout the night, and have nightmares or difficulty waking up. Wanting to sleep with a parent does not signal a shift in sleep patterns; it is a common response after a death, reflecting the need for reassurance at the end of the day, when children often feel vulnerable, tired, and scared.

Shift in Play Patterns

Play may become either very aggressive or passive. Children might change in their ability to share or play cooperatively or in their desire to be with other children. It is not cause for concern if children have an exaggerated response to small losses or express feelings of grief through play. It is normal for them to play out recurrent themes related to a death in an attempt to understand what has occurred.

Shift in Expression of Feelings

Children may become more anxious over time, responding with fear or frequent startle behavior. Rapid shifts in mood and the intensity of the expression of feelings can be areas for concern.

Shift in Eating Patterns

There can be either a significant decrease or increase in eating. It is important not to be judgmental as this change is part of the child's attempt to cope with stress and feelings of loss. If eating does not normalize over time and the child begins to gain or lose a significant amount of weight, consultation with a physician and a mental health practitioner would be appropriate.

Inability to Separate

Difficulty with separation is a normal response to grief. If it extends beyond a six-month period and involves severe anxiety, fear, and tantrums, it would be an area of concern.

Shift in School Performance

Initially, children's concentration may be compromised in school. If they do not regain their focus over time, it is a signal to seek help and explore the difficulty. This area can be verified with teachers by comparing academic and behavioral performance before and after the death.

Dear Kids,

This book was written to help you take time to think about yourself, to create, and to remember your loved one. After the death of a loved one, people have different feelings and experiences. These activities will give you many ways to show what you feel and experience, which may be hard for you to put into words.

The book is like a journal, where you can record your thoughts, feelings, and memories about this time. You can work on it slowly or finish it quickly. You can choose where you want to begin and move from page to page. It can be saved for the future and looked at to remember what you have been through and how much you have done to help yourself.

—Erika and Ellen

For You to Think About

It is important to know that change is a part of life. There are many things that change in your life, and no matter how hard it may seem at first, over time you will adjust to those changes.

People and things change. Some changes happen quickly and some so slowly you might not even notice them happening. There are things you can change, like your hairstyle, and things you can't change, like the size of your feet. There are changes you may want, like turning a year older. There are also changes you probably don't want, like a friend moving to another town. There are small changes, like the length of days as the season moves from winter to spring to summer to fall. There are also big changes that may feel like a tornado, leaving many things turned upside down and confused.

You have had many changes in your life. You can look at your baby pictures and see how your face and body have changed. As you learn more and more, in school or from other people, your mind has changed, too.

Directions

Draw pictures or find photographs of yourself as a baby, as a very young child, and now. Place them in the doorways below.

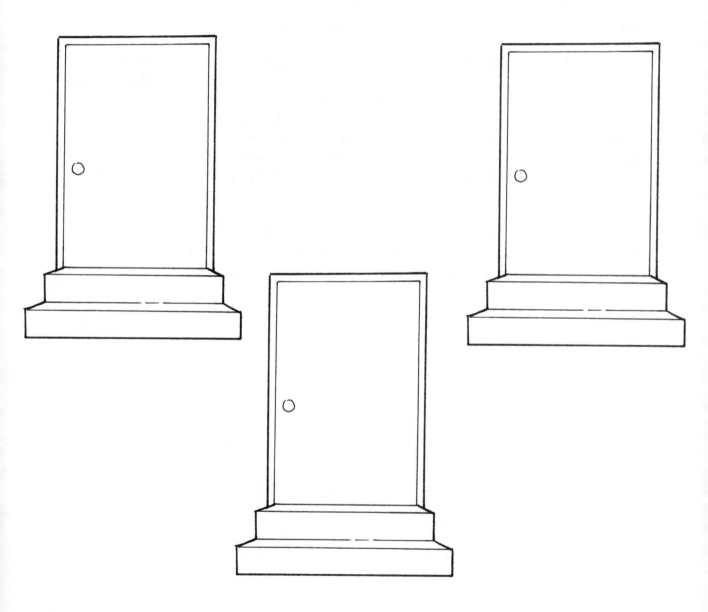

Why Did You Die?

Questions

From picture to picture, how have you changed?

_____

_____

_____

What do you like about the ways you have changed?

_____

_____

_____

Is there anything you don't like about these changes?

_____

_____

_____

What are some of the reasons for these changes?

_____

_____

_____

Activity 2   Changes You Can Control and Changes You Can't

For You to Think About

You can control some changes in life. For example, when your favorite TV program is over and the next program is scary, you can change the channel or turn the TV off. There are also many changes you can't control, like the death of someone you love.

Mariana had always loved dancing. Every Tuesday after school, she went to a hip-hop class and practiced the steps in front of her mirror at home. Her friend Jessie went to a tap class that she really loved and was so excited about it that Mariana decided to change classes. She could hardly wait to start her new lessons.

On the day of her first tap class, Mariana's father dropped her off at dancing school. When he came to pick her up, he saw Mariana crying as she walked away from the girls in the class. As they drove home, Mariana explained that the other girls had asked why her mother hadn't driven her to class. They didn't know that Mariana's mother had died last month. So much had changed in her family that Mariana didn't feel ready to answer the question or know what to say.

Mariana's father agreed that there had been many changes in her life. Some kinds of change were good, and some weren't. Some she could control, like deciding to take tap instead of hip-hop, and some she couldn't. Her mother's death was a change she couldn't control. Mariana and her father talked about what she could say if she didn't want to answer questions about her mother. Together, they decided that she would say, "My mother died, and it's something I don't want to talk about." Then she would change the topic of conversation.

When she realized that she could decide how to respond to questions, Mariana felt more in control, which helped her feel more comfortable.

Directions

Change the image of this butterfly by creating a collage. You can tear colored construction paper or magazine pictures into tiny pieces and glue them onto the butterfly.

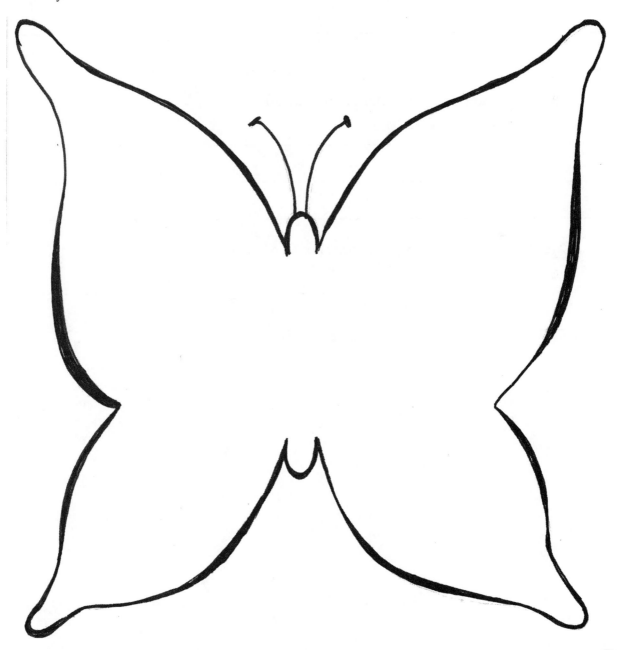

Questions

What do you like about how you changed the butterfly?

_____

_____

_____

What are three things you can change in your life?

_____

_____

_____

What are three things you can't change about your life?

_____

_____

_____

For You to Think About

When you look in a mirror, you see the outside of yourself, which is how other people see you. Inside, you may feel very different. Things that have happened to you, what other people have said, how you feel, and what you think are all part of how you feel inside.

Alexandra hated going to school because her best friend, Sydney, had recently died. She cried every morning when it was time to get ready for school. As she got dressed, she would scream about her socks being too tight or her pants being too short. Her mother could tell that something was really bothering Alexandra, and they talked about how hard it had been since Sydney died. As her mother cuddled her, Alexandra cried and said, "I miss Sydney. There isn't anyone else to play with in school."

In the classroom, Alexandra smiled and followed all the directions. She worked hard and kept her uncomfortable feelings inside. Her teacher never saw the sad, angry, scared, and frustrated feelings behind Alexandra's smiling face.

Directions

Decorate the mask on the left to show how you think people see you. Decorate the mask on the right to show how you see yourself.

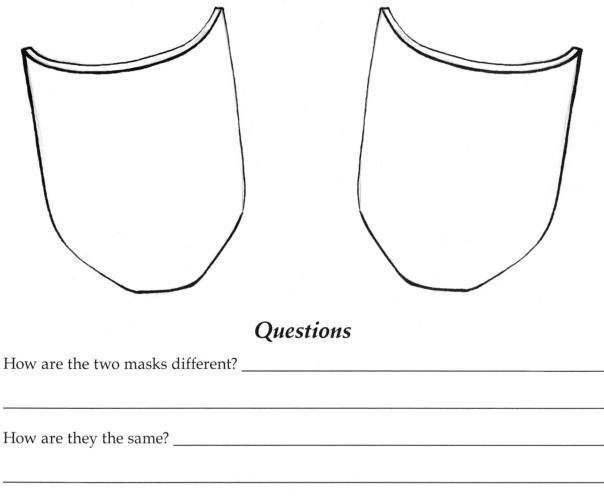

Questions

How are the two masks different? _____

_____

How are they the same? _____

_____

Do you like one more than the other? If so, which do you like better, and why?

_____

_____

You Have Many Feelings

Activity 4

For You to Think About

Your feelings change all the time—every day, every hour, and sometimes even by the minute. You can even have more than one feeling at the same time. You may worry that uncomfortable feelings—like anger, sadness, and fear—won't go away, but they always do. Talking about your feelings and trying to understand them can help a lot.

When his uncle died, Michael knew that he felt sad. Uncle Leo had been his buddy, and they had spent lots of time together, fishing, riding bikes, and just hanging out. At first, Michael missed Uncle Leo very much, but after a while it seemed like he stopped missing him. Then one night at dinner, Michael yelled at his sister when she didn't pass him the ketchup right away. When his dad told him it was time to brush his teeth, Michael began to shout and kick the furniture. Michael didn't know why he was so upset and didn't like feeling that out of control.

His mother asked if he often thought about Uncle Leo. Michael didn't want to talk about him and just said, "I hate Uncle Leo, and I don't care that he died!" Michael felt mad at his uncle, but he didn't want to admit it. He thought he was supposed to be sad, not angry. How could he hate his favorite uncle? His mother reassured him, "It's okay to be angry. I'm angry, too. I'm mad that my brother left me." She said there would be times when Michael would feel angry or sad or confused, and there would also be times when he would feel happy remembering Uncle Leo. Talking about his feelings helped Michael, and he smiled as he answered, "Yeah, remember the time Uncle Leo threw me into the pool?" Michael and his mother laughed as she wished him a good night's sleep.

Directions

Think about all the different feelings you had today and choose four. Select a color to represent each feeling and fill in one of the rectangles with that color. Write the feeling on the line below the rectangle. Then use these four colors to create a design in the circle that shows the mix of your feelings.

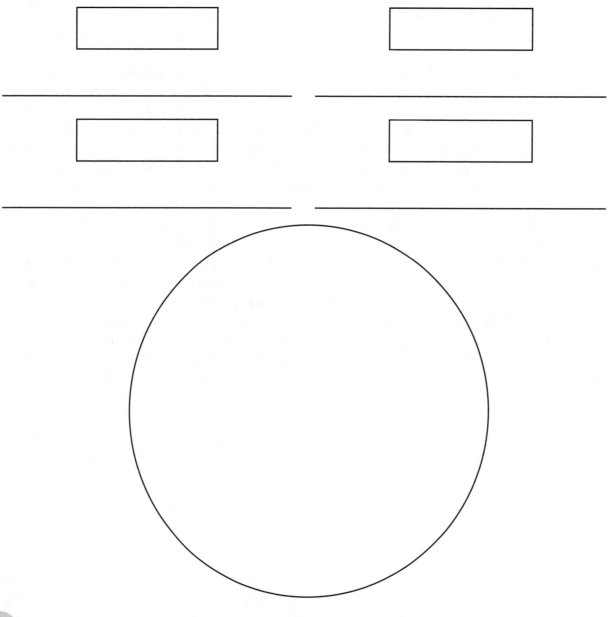

Questions

What is your favorite feeling? Why?

_____

_____

_____

What is your least favorite feeling? Why?

_____

_____

_____

What do you feel right now?

_____

_____

_____

Write about one of the feelings you had today.

_____

_____

_____

_____

Activity 5   Your Life Is a Journey

For You to Think About

One way to picture your life is as a journey or lifeline. On this journey, you will meet many people who are important to you. Some of them may be in your life for only a short time, and it may even be hard for you to remember some of them, but they are all part of your lifeline.

Serena was eight years old when she created her lifeline. It was like a ruler that had lines for every year of her life instead of inches. Near each number, she wrote about, or drew, important people who had come into her life that year. Her mother was the first person on her lifeline, even though Serena didn't remember her; she had died when Serena was very young. Then she drew the babysitter who had cared for her until she was two. Serena had heard many stories about these two women, and she knew how much they had cared about her.

The other people Serena chose to include were her second-grade teacher, her best friend, and her scout leader. These people were very important to Serena—especially her best friend, who recently moved to town. Some of them had been part of her life for only a short time and some for a long time. Some had joined her on her journey when she was very young and some recently. They had something in common: they all cared about Serena, and she cared about all of them.

Directions

Along this lifeline, draw or write about important people in your life. Show how old you were when these people came into your life.

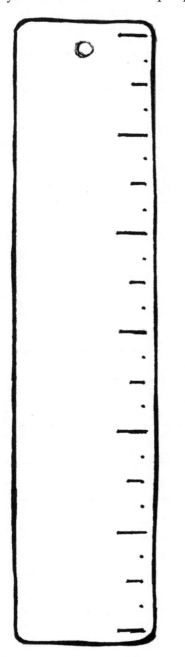

Questions

Which person on your lifeline is most important to you, and why?

_____

_____

_____

_____

What do you like about the lifeline you created?

_____

_____

_____

_____

Who do you think you might add to your lifeline when you are a grown-up?

_____

_____

_____

_____

_____

For You to Think About

There are many people who care about you. Some of these people may be family members, friends, teachers, or members of your community. They may be people you see every day or people you don't see often. These people are called your "support system," which is a group of people who care about you and want to help you. Thinking about these people can help you remember that you are not alone.

When Alison's dog, Jake, died, she felt very sad and lonely. She began crying in class the next day, and her teacher took her aside to ask what was wrong. Speaking with her teacher helped Alison feel calmer, and she was able to get through the morning. At lunchtime, Alison felt sad again, so she told her friend Lauren about Jake. Lauren had had a hamster that died, and the two girls shared stories. Again, Alison felt better. That night her grandparents made a special visit to have dinner with her. Alison realized that many people cared about her and would talk with her about Jake. When she went to sleep that night, Alison thought about her dog, but she also thought about her teacher, her friend, and her family.

Directions

Think about the people who are part of your support system. In the box below, draw a solar system with yourself in the center. Add as many planets as you need, and write the name of a person who cares about you in each one.

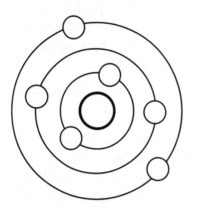

Questions

How does each person show that they care for you?

_____

_____

_____

_____

_____

_____

_____

What do you feel when you look at this solar system?

_____

_____

_____

_____

_____

_____

_____

Activity 7   Every Family Is Unique

For You to Think About

Everyone's family is different. People come from different countries, speak different languages, follow different religions, have different shades of skin color, and live in different communities. Some children live with their birth parents, some are adopted, some live with one parent, and some live with other family members or friends.

In art class, Lilly had to make a drawing of her family. She felt uncomfortable because she thought her family was not like other families. Instead of drawing her family, Lilly made herself feel better by drawing a beautiful lake with mountains. Her teacher said that Lilly's picture was lovely, but she hadn't followed directions and needed to draw her family. Feeling angry, scared, and embarrassed, Lilly quickly drew herself and her mother.

All the students' pictures were put up on the bulletin board. Lilly's picture was messy, and she was very sorry she hadn't drawn it more carefully. Looking at the different drawings, Lilly realized something very important: each picture was different because each family was different. Hugo lived with his mother, father, brother, and aunt. Dena lived with her father and grandparents. Lilly lived with just her mother, and that was okay!

Directions

Imagine you are creating a family crest to show the history of your family. In the outline below, make a collage that represents your family. You can use magazine images, photographs, and your own drawings.

Activities to Help Children Cope with Grief and Loss

Questions

Is anyone or anything missing from your family crest?

_____

_____

_____

_____

What do you like about the crest you have created?

_____

_____

_____

_____

Choose three items you included and tell how each represents your family.

_____

_____

_____

_____

_____

_____

_____

A Special Place Can Feel Good

For You to Think About

There are places you have been and places you might like to visit. Some of these places are more special to you than others. Remembering these special places or thinking about going somewhere special can often change how you feel.

When you are feeling sad, upset, or angry, there are ways to help you change how you feel. One way is to think about a place that is special to you. Even if you can't actually go to this place, you can travel there in your imagination.

Choose a place where you feel very comfortable and happy. It might be somewhere you went on vacation, your room, or the beach. It can be a real place or an imaginary place.

Now, get yourself into a comfortable position, perhaps in a chair, on the sofa, or lying on the floor. Let your arms rest gently by your side. Take slow and easy breaths. Close your eyes, if that is comfortable for you. Imagine you are a limp noodle, and relax each part of your body.

Think about your special place. Are you there alone or did you take someone with you? What do you see? Are there colors or objects? Take some time just to look. Then listen to all the sounds and breathe in the smells. Notice how this place makes you feel. When you are ready, leave your special place and take the calm feelings with you. Remember that this place will always be there for you. You can go back at any time.

Directions

Draw your special place with you in it. If you prefer, you can use a photograph of yourself. Cut the background off, paste your image in the box below, and create a new background.

Questions

How does this picture make you feel?

_____

_____

_____

_____

What are you doing in the picture?

_____

_____

_____

_____

Where is your special place?

_____

_____

_____

_____

Activity 9

A Gift from Your Loved One

For You to Think About

When someone we love has given us a gift, it is nice to carry it with us. The person who died gave you gifts that you can carry. These gifts may be things you can actually touch or feelings you hold inside yourself. Holding something from your loved one can make you feel good.

School was over, and summer was finally here. For the past three years, Julia had gone to summer camp, and she had always enjoyed it. This summer she didn't want to go. The night before she was supposed to leave, Julia cried and pleaded not to go. Every summer before, her grandmother had waited with her for the camp bus and had been there to pick her up. But her grandmother had died a month ago, and Julia missed her so much.

Julia told her mother that she was afraid to go to camp. Her mother sat with her, and they talked about her fears. Even though her mother promised to wait for the bus with her, Julia still wanted her grandmother, who had loved her and made everything feel okay. Julia said, "Nobody can make me feel the way Grandma did." Julia's mother said she would be right back, and she returned with a surprise. She gave Julia her grandmother's watch, the one that her grandmother had worn every day.

The next morning, Julia got onto the bus with the watch safely zipped in the pocket of her backpack. Whenever she felt scared or lonely, she hugged the backpack tightly. Knowing that her grandmother's watch was inside made her feel much better.

Directions

In the space below, create a picture of a gift from your loved one. It can be an object or a design of your feelings. You can cut it out and carry it with you or put it somewhere you can easily look at it when you want to.

Activity 9   A Gift from Your Loved One

Questions

What gift did your loved one give you?

_____

_____

_____

_____

_____

How does this picture make you feel?

_____

_____

_____

_____

Where would you like to keep it?

_____

_____

_____

_____

Everything Has a Life Span   Activity 10

For You to Think About

Every living thing has a life span and dies someday. Some life spans are shorter than others. Insects may live for only a few days, while people can live as long as one hundred years and trees can live for hundreds of years.

When Zachary was born, a cat named Junior already lived with his mother and father. Zachary's first word was "kitty." When he began to walk, Zachary followed Junior everywhere. When he was older, he would sneak up and say, "Boo," and then laugh as Junior jumped. Junior slept in Zachary's room at night. When Zachary was seven, Junior died. Junior had lived for twenty years, which is a very long life for a cat. Zachary missed Junior terribly. He cried a lot and asked, "Why did Junior die?" He felt empty and sad without his special friend. Although Zachary understood that his cat had lived a long life, he wanted Junior to stay with him forever. His mother explained that it just wasn't possible; every living thing dies someday. She told Zachary that he would have a lot of feelings about Junior's death, and suggested that he think about his wonderful memories of Junior. Zachary told his mom that he would never forget Junior.

Directions

The pictures below show three stages in the life span of a chicken. In the empty boxes on the next page, draw a picture of three stages in the life span of another living thing.

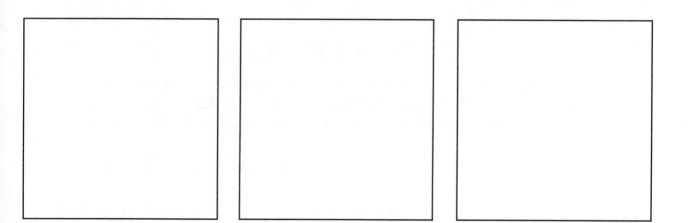

Questions

How long is the life span of the living thing you drew?

_____

How did it change from drawing to drawing?

_____

_____

_____

What stage of its life span is your favorite, and why?

_____

_____

_____

_____

_____

_____

There Are Many Causes of Death

For You to Think About

There are many different causes of death, but people's words or thoughts never cause death. Nothing you said or thought was the reason why your loved one died.

All living things–plants, animals, and people–die. When it doesn't rain for a long time, plants outside may die. A forest fire can kill animals and plants. The fire may be caused by natural forces, such as lightning, or by an accident, such as a burning match that is dropped.

Most people die when they get very old, but this is not always what happens. Some people die in accidents, and others kill themselves. There are people who die from drug overdoses or in war. Certain illnesses can cause people to die, too.

There was a cause for your loved one's death, but it was not anything you said or thought.

Directions

In the boxes below, draw two things that can cause death.

Questions

How can these things cause death?

_____

_____

_____

_____

_____

Have you ever seen anything like what you have drawn? If you have, describe when and where. If you haven't, describe how you got this idea.

_____

_____

_____

_____

_____

Can you think of other things that can make a living thing die?

_____

_____

_____

_____

How Your Loved One Died   Activity 12

Yoon and Kyongok were home with their parents. Their father had not been feeling well and was taking a nap. As he slept, he made unusual snoring noises. Their mother woke him twice to ask if he was feeling all right, and each time he answered, "I'm just tired."

Suddenly, the kids heard their mother yelling at them to go downstairs as she dialed 911. Their father was rushed to the hospital, and the children followed in their grandmother's car. They waited in a small room, and soon their mother arrived with a counselor. Kyongok immediately asked, "What happened to Dad? Is he okay?" "Your father is with Aunt Kim in heaven," their mother answered. Yoon and Kyongok began crying.

After a while, the counselor asked if there were questions the children wanted answered. Yoon asked three important questions:

1. How did my father die?
2. Would he have lived if the ambulance came sooner?
3. Could I have done anything to help prevent my father's death?

The counselor asked an emergency-room nurse to answer them. He explained that their father's heart had stopped beating. When a person's heart stops beating, it can no longer pump blood to bring oxygen to his brain and other organs, and he dies. Even if the ambulance had come sooner, it would not have saved their father's life because he had already died. The answer to Yoon's last question was the most painful. Although the children and their mother wished they could have done something to save him, that was not possible. They did not know something was wrong with his heart because they weren't doctors.

Understanding what had happened helped Yoon, Kyongok, and their mother grieve without feeling guilty or ashamed.

Directions

In the space below, write what you know about your loved one's death. Here are some things you can include:

- How old your loved one was
- Your loved one's name and what you called him or her
- The date of death
- What happened at that time
- What caused the death

Questions

Is there any more information you would like to add to what you wrote?

_____

_____

_____

_____

Did this activity bring back any memories? Can you write one down?

_____

_____

_____

Do you have any questions you would like answered about the death?

_____

_____

_____

Whom can you go to for answers to your questions?

_____

If you shared what you know about your loved one's death with your friends, how do you think they would respond?

_____

Activity 13

Special Things You Did with Your Loved One

For You to Think About

Some of the things you did with your loved one are special. These might be things you shared in common, enjoyed doing together, or taught one another. Memories of these special things will stay with you forever.

Crystal and Richard played a special game together almost every morning. They slid down the hallway on the linoleum floor to see who could get the farthest. They loved this game and could make one another laugh just by saying, "Slide" with a sly smile.

After Richard died, Crystal still played their game. She pretended they were together while she slid down the hall. Years later, when she babysat for her cousins, Crystal taught them how to play. She told them about the fun she and Richard had had playing the game.

Directions

Draw a picture of you and your loved one doing something special together.

Questions

What were some of the special things you and your loved one did together?

_____

_____

_____

_____

_____

_____

Describe when and where you did these things.

_____

_____

_____

_____

What was the best part about doing them?

_____

_____

_____

_____

Activity 14

What Your Loved One Enjoyed

For You to Think About

There are certain things that made your loved one happy, such as favorite activities, people, food, clothing, or places. You can create wonderful memories by thinking about these things.

Melody's little brother Joshua was three years old when he drowned in a terrible accident. The family grieved for a long time and always felt the sadness of not having Joshua with them. A few years later, Melody's parents had another baby. They named him Daniel. To help Daniel know Joshua better, Melody and her parents made a book about him. This book was filled with stories about how Joshua loved pizza and watched his favorite movies again and again. They included silly things Joshua had said, and each wrote what they loved most about him. Joshua would always be a part of their family, even if he could no longer be touched or held. His brother, sister, and parents would always feel him in their hearts.

What Your Loved One Enjoyed Activity 14

Directions

Make a collage that shows the things your loved one enjoyed most. You can use magazine pictures, photographs, wrappers, drawings, or anything else that can fit on this page.

Questions

Do you enjoy any of these things?

_____

_____

_____

_____

_____

Do you dislike any of these things?

_____

_____

_____

_____

Which of these things did you enjoy together?

_____

_____

_____

_____

The Idea of Death Looks Different to Each of Us

Activity 15

For You to Think About

When someone dies, it is hard to think about how and why it happened. For some people, imagining death as a character, like the Grim Reaper or a skeleton, helps to make the experience real. Many people picture death as scary, and other people see it as peaceful.

Kenya, Wanda, and Harry each had a very special person who died. At a meeting of their bereavement group, they created images of what they thought death would look like and then described what their symbols meant.

Kenya drew a ghostlike figure that represented the cancer that caused her mother to die. Wanda used clay to sculpt a creature with long tentacles and described how it quickly swept her friend away. Harry drew the headstone at his grandfather's grave. He talked about how during the funeral he realized his grandfather was dead, and he described the pain he felt in his chest.

Directions

Draw a character or creature that shows what death looks like.

Activity 15

Questions

Describe your character or creature.

_____

_____

_____

_____

_____

_____

If it could talk, what would it say?

_____

_____

_____

_____

What would you say back to it?

_____

_____

_____

_____

Illnesses, Accidents, and Natural Events

For You to Think About

Most people do not want to die, but death is often caused by things that can't be controlled, such as illnesses, accidents, or natural events.

Some illnesses are life threatening, like cancer or AIDS. If they are not treated with strong medicines, they can cause death. Sometimes, even strong medicine doesn't help. The illness spreads through the person's body, stopping it from working, and the person dies.

Chronic illnesses, like sickle cell anemia, diabetes, and emphysema, are other causes of death. People with chronic illnesses have something wrong with their bodies that scientists and doctors can't cure. These illnesses may occur before birth or develop later in life. People who have these illnesses need medicine to live, and they may look unhealthy or seem to suffer.

An acute illness is one that happens suddenly. Not all acute illnesses are serious. Some, like pneumonia or infections that spread inside a person's body, can become serious enough to cause death and usually require the person to be hospitalized.

There are also mental illnesses, like severe depression, that can cause people a tremendous amount of suffering. People with these illnesses may feel hopeless and think it would be better to die than to continue living. When the illness is not controlled by prescribed medication, some people suffer so badly that they commit suicide.

People also die of causes other than illness. Accidents, like being hit by a car or falling from a high place, can kill people. People die in wars, and sometimes one person kills another on purpose. Events in nature, like tornadoes or tsunamis, also cause deaths.

It can help you to remember that, no matter what the cause of death, your loved one would not have chosen to die if he or she had control over it.

Directions

List five things that are difficult to control and can cause harm.

1. _____

2. _____

3. _____

4. _____

5. _____

In the space below, draw a picture of one of these things.

Questions

Have you ever seen this thing happen?

_____

What words would you use to describe it?

_____

_____

_____

_____

_____

How would you protect yourself from it?

_____

_____

_____

_____

_____

Activity 17

Death Stops the Body from Working

Sally was very upset after her cousin Michael died. When it was time to go to the funeral, she cried very hard. Her parents asked what was wrong. Sally said, "I'm worried that Michael will be cold, and I know he's alone in the dark. What will happen when his coffin is buried?" Her parents reassured Sally that her cousin's body did not work any longer. He could not feel cold, and he could not see where he was or if it was dark.

Directions

List all the body parts you can think of that keep people alive. Next to each part, write what you know about how it works.

_____

_____

_____

_____

_____

_____

_____

_____

Questions

Write any questions you have about how the body works.

_____

_____

_____

_____

_____

Are there questions you have about what caused your loved one's body to stop working?

_____

_____

_____

_____

Did you ever have questions about what happened to the body after your loved one died?

_____

_____

_____

> ## *For You to Think About*
>
> There are things we know that don't cause death. There is nothing someone could say that can cause someone to die. There is no thought that can cause a death. No one's feelings can make someone die. It is important to remember that nothing you said, thought, or felt made your loved one die. If you have questions about why the death happened, share them with an adult who can understand and explain what really happened.

Sammy drew a picture of his family together in the kitchen. In one corner, there was a big, messy trashcan, overflowing with garbage. When his counselor asked about what he had drawn, Sammy said, "I should have taken out the garbage because that's how my sister got cancer." Sammy had heard his parents and the neighbors talking about their community being built on land that had been filled in over a huge mountain of garbage. They had described the garbage as toxic waste, which meant it was poisonous. Sammy had heard part of this conversation, and he thought that if he had emptied the trashcan his sister wouldn't have gotten cancer and died. He was very relieved when he found out he was not responsible for her cancer.

Directions

Did you ever wonder if anything you did caused your loved one's death? Draw a picture that shows what you thought about.

Questions

Can you think of anything else that doesn't cause death?

_____

_____

Is there anything you would like to know about death?

_____

_____

Activity 19   The Funeral Service

For You to Think About

A funeral or service for the loved one is a time that family and friends get together to say good-bye to the body of the person who died. It is also a time to remember and talk about a loved one's life.

When Sophia, Katrina, and Cristina's neighbor Mr. Clark died, their mom asked them if they wanted to go to the funeral service. She said that it was their decision and it would be okay if they chose to stay home. The girls had felt very close to Mr. Clark and were sad about his death. But they had never been to a funeral and they worried about what it would be like. Their mother explained that it was a sad event, and many people there might be crying. Mr. Clark's body would be in a coffin, which might be open. If it were open, people at the service would be able to see the body. It wouldn't move, and it might look gray or pale.

Sophia, Katrina, and Cristina decided that they wanted to go. They wanted to see what would happen and listen to what people said. They wanted to say good-bye to Mr. Clark. Before the funeral, the girls took their favorite photographs of him and pasted them on a poster board. They brought the poster to the funeral, along with colored pencils, markers, and stickers. Before the funeral service, they added words and designs to their poster and invited other people to write about Mr. Clark, too. It made them feel as if they were part of the funeral service, with something special to share.

Why Did You Die?

Directions

In the space below, create a collage that will help you remember your loved one's funeral. You can include cards, obituaries, items from the funeral home, pictures from magazines, or your own drawings.

Questions

What memories came to your mind while creating the collage?

_____

_____

_____

Did you leave out anything you would like to include? You can go back and add to your collage.

_____

What are some feelings you had at the funeral?

_____

_____

What feelings do you think other people had?

_____

_____

_____

Did you say anything during the service? If you did, what did you say? If you didn't, is there anything you would like to have said?

_____

_____

_____

People Give Gifts to Show They Care

For You to Think About

When someone dies, many people take or send gifts to the family. Often, these gifts are flowers or food. People often send cards, too. These cards are called sympathy cards. These gifts and cards are a way to tell the family that others are sorry the person died and that they understand it is a time of sadness.

Bobby wanted to show his friend Evan how sorry he was that Evan's brother had died. His parents had sent a fruit basket to Evan's family, but Bobby wanted to do something just for his friend. Bobby made a card to give Evan. First, he drew a picture with markers, but then he didn't know what to write inside. He couldn't think of a way to show his feelings. None of the words he thought of seemed right, and yet he wanted Evan to know that he cared. After some time, he decided to just write this:

Dear Evan,

I wish your brother didn't die.
I'm sorry that you are sad.

From,

Bobby

The next day, Bobby gave Evan the card. Evan still felt sad, but he knew that he had a really good friend.

People Give Gifts to
Show They Care

Directions

Draw a gift or the outside of a sympathy card that will let someone know you care.

Why Did You Die?

Questions

Where would you like to keep what you have created?

_____

What would you write to go along with your gift or card?

_____

_____

_____

_____

_____

Do you remember any cards or gifts that were special to you?

_____

_____

_____

Activity 21

A Place People Go to Remember

For You to Think About

After the funeral, the body is taken to a special place. It may be a cemetery, a mausoleum, or another specific place decided upon by the family. People can go to this place to help them remember their loved one.

Nora, Eddie, and Tyrone all went to a support group for children who had had someone they love die. Their group leader asked each of them where the body of their loved one was. Nora said, "In the ground in the cemetery, and my mom goes there every day." Tyrone said, "In the mausoleum, in a wall." Eddie said, "My grandma's ashes were put in a special garden."

They were each surprised at the others' answers. Their group leader reminded them that they didn't need to worry, no matter what special place the family had chosen. The person's body no longer felt pain. It didn't sense heat or cold, and it didn't need food or air. What was important was that friends and family could go to this place to remember their loved one.

Directions

Draw a picture or take a photograph of this place, and put it in the frame below.

Questions

Have you been to this place? _____

If you have, what did you do while you were there?

_____

_____

_____

_____

_____

If you haven't, would you like to go? What do you think you would do there? Would you like to take anything there? If so, what?

_____

_____

_____

_____

_____

_____

Beliefs About What Happens After Death

For You to Think About

People have different thoughts and beliefs about what happens after death. Some people believe in heaven and some in reincarnation. Some people are not sure about what happens, and others think that nothing happens. It can be comforting to think about what has happened to your loved one.

Katie believed her friend's spirit was in heaven. Annie described her father as a bird in the sky. Todd shared that his brother's spirit was with him in their bedroom. Justin thought all these ideas were silly and said that his grandmother was dead in her coffin underground. Their counselor, Ms. Martinez, told them that there were no right or wrong answers to the question of what happens after death. She explained that every religion has its own beliefs. Some religions believe the spirit or soul goes to heaven. Some religions believe in reincarnation, which means that people come back to Earth in a different body. Other religions believe there is a place where someone's spirit waits before joining God. Some people don't believe in spirits, souls, or God at all.

Ms. Martinez asked Katie, Annie, Todd, and Justin what was important to remember about other people's beliefs. Here is what they said:

- No one knows for sure what happens after death.
- It is important to be tolerant of other people's beliefs, even if they are different from yours.
- When someone dies, those who cared about that person suffer.
- It is important to be kind to people who have lost a loved one.

Beliefs About What Happens After Death

Directions

Draw a picture of where you think your loved one is now.

Questions

What are your feelings about what you have drawn?

_____

_____

_____

_____

_____

Is there anyone else there?

_____

Describe the place you have drawn.

_____

_____

_____

_____

_____

_____

_____

Activity 23

Keeping a Feeling of Togetherness

For You to Think About

When a loved one dies, you can still feel a sense of togetherness with that person. It is important to remember you cannot actually join the person you loved. However, you can choose to imagine your loved one with you at different times and places.

When Shelly and Sharon's grandmother died unexpectedly, the girls and their parents had a difficult time. Their family was shocked. After their feelings of shock went away, they met with a counselor to share their emotions. Each of them talked about special moments when they could feel Grandma with them. They wondered if it was their imagination or if they were sensing Grandma's presence or spirit nearby. They were comforted by this sensation and liked the idea that, even after her death, they could still feel Grandma in their lives.

Erin's uncle committed suicide after struggling with a mental illness for many years. Erin missed him a lot. Her aunt told Erin she could choose something of her uncle's to keep. Erin chose a box of playing cards. Her uncle had taught her to play solitaire, and the cards were special to her. Every time she played with them, Erin imagined her uncle sitting next to her. She would smile, remembering their jokes about the Queen of Hearts eating tarts.

Why Did You Die?

Directions

Complete this story by writing about how Lauren kept a sense of being together with her father after he died.

Lauren's dad died when she was seven years old. _____

_____

_____

_____

_____

_____

_____

_____

_____

_____

_____

_____

_____

Questions

What title would you give this story?

_____

_____

How does this story make you feel?

_____

_____

_____

_____

_____

How do you think sensing togetherness with her father made Lauren feel?

_____

_____

_____

_____

_____

For You to Think About

After the death of a loved one, you may experience painful feelings, like anger, sadness, guilt, and loneliness. These emotions may come and go. They can change depending on how recent the death was, where you are, whom you are with, and what is happening in your life. Talking about these feelings can help.

Lisette's sister Joan died five years ago when she was thirteen and Lisette was eight. Joan had been sick for a few years before her death. At the time of Joan's death, Lisette had many feelings. One part of her didn't believe it was real. Joan had been in the hospital so many times during those years, but she had always come home. Lisette was sure that this time would be like all the others. Another part of Lisette knew that it was real and that Joan would not be coming home again.

As time passed, Lisette found that she had a whole range of emotions, including some she had never experienced before. She was mad at Joan for leaving her, confused about why she had to die, sad that she would never be able to hug her sister again, lonely, and disappointed that her parents didn't seem to pay any attention to her anymore. Talking with Ms. Vega, her counselor, Lisette found ways to express these painful feelings of grief. Lisette felt better, although she realized that she would always miss Joan.

Some years later, Lisette was no longer enjoying her life. She didn't want to be with her friends; she just wanted to stay home. She was feeling anxious and depressed. Lisette's mother suggested that she talk with her counselor again. Ms. Vega hadn't seen Lisette for some time and asked how old she was. Lisette answered, "Twelve, but next week is my birthday." "And how old was Joan when she died?" Ms. Vega asked. "Thirteen," Joan said.

Turning the same age that her sister had been when she died was very powerful for Lisette. All her feelings came rushing back, overwhelming her. She realized that she was afraid she would be diagnosed with a serious illness and die, too. Lisette and Ms. Vega talked about these feelings and fears. The counselor helped Lisette understand that her sorrow might reappear at different times. It wouldn't end, but it would change as Lisette changed. Major events, like her high school graduation, might make Lisette miss Joan very much. Ms. Vega said that it was important for Lisette to pay attention to her feelings and reach out for help when she needed it, the way she had this time.

Feelings of Grief Can Change

Directions

After the death of someone you love, your feelings of grief may seem like a spiral, going around and around. On the spiral below, show where you were at the beginning of your grief and where you are now. Place all the different feelings you have had along the spiral. You can add colors, lines, and shapes, too.

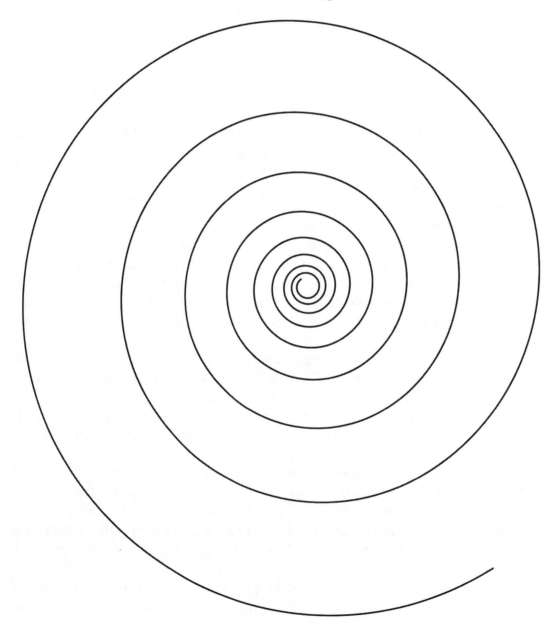

Questions

Describe where you are in the spiral.

_____

_____

_____

_____

_____

How do you think your feelings will change?

_____

_____

_____

What feelings have you had most often?

_____

_____

_____

_____

_____

Activity 25 People Grieve Differently

For You to Think About

People who are grieving have many different feelings. They may be angry or sad. They may feel guilty or lonely without their loved one. They also have different ways of showing these feelings. Some people will show their feelings through actions, some through words, and some through moods.

When Anthony's father died, his older sister, Maria, didn't want to talk about it. She just stayed in her room. His grandfather was so angry that he slammed his hand on the kitchen table and broke a plate. His mother cried and cried, which scared Anthony.

After the funeral, many people came to visit his family. There was a lot of food and noise in the house. Some of the visitors talked on and on, and some were even laughing. Others cried and hugged Anthony. Anthony himself was sad, but at the same time, he wanted to play with his cousins.

Anthony had never seen people express so many emotions in so many different ways.

Directions

Draw a picture of a person or a group of people grieving.

Questions

Describe what you have drawn.

_____

_____

_____

_____

_____

Do you know anyone who has grieved in this way?

_____

What other ways have you seen people grieve?

_____

_____

_____

_____

_____

_____

_____

Wishing Things Could Be Different

For You to Think About

People often wish that things could be different, even when they know their wishes can't come true.

Carrie imagined that there was a genie who could make her wishes come true. She wished she had a million dollars. She wished it would always be summer. She wished for world peace. And after her aunt died, Carrie wished that her aunt were still alive.

Carrie told her dad about her imaginary genie. Her father said that he had many wishes, too. He knew that some of his wishes could come true and some couldn't. Carrie and her dad agreed that it still felt good to wish—even when they knew their wishes couldn't come true.

Directions

In the space below, draw a picture of something you wish for that you know can come true.

Questions

Have you ever wished your loved one was still alive?

_____

What is one wish you have that you know can't come true?

_____

_____

_____

_____

_____

How do you feel when you think about that wish?

_____

_____

_____

_____

_____

For You to Think About

You will think about your loved one at different times. It may happen when you hear a song you both liked, when you taste a food you enjoyed together, or when you smell a familiar aroma. These thoughts may simply pop into your mind. You can also choose a special place and time to think about your loved one.

Diana had always been a good student who looked forward to school every day. After her younger brother Jorge was killed in a car accident, she dreaded going to school. Before Jorge died, Diana had walked him to and from school and talked with him at lunchtime. Now she went to school by herself, and she missed taking care of her brother. Sometimes, in the middle of class, her sad feelings filled her and she couldn't concentrate on her schoolwork. Her teacher arranged for Diana to be able to go the nurse's office when she felt this way. Sometimes she talked with the nurse, and sometimes she just sat there quietly. It helped Diana to know that she had a special place to go. She could think about Jorge, cry, and let herself feel her feelings. Then she was able to return to class, focus on her work, and be with her schoolmates.

Directions

For one week, keep a record of what you were doing each time you thought about your loved one.

Day	What I Was Doing
_____	_____
	_____
	_____
	_____
_____	_____
	_____
	_____
	_____
_____	_____
	_____
	_____
	_____

Day	What I Was Doing
_____	_____
	_____
	_____
	_____
_____	_____
	_____
	_____
	_____
_____	_____
	_____
	_____
	_____
_____	_____
	_____
	_____
	_____

Questions

Were you surprised by anything you wrote?

_____

_____

_____

What are the things that remind you of your loved one?

_____

_____

_____

_____

_____

_____

_____

_____

Pretending to Be a Superhero

For You to Think About

Many people wish they had superpowers and could stop terrible things from happening. These powers could blow away illness and protect people from accidents. Pretending we can change things through superpowers can be fun, even when we know that things really won't change.

Jamal loved playing with his action figures. When he visited his mother in the hospital, he would pretend that he was fighting evil with the help of Dr. Batman and Nurse Robin. They would fly around the room, giving out magic medicine to make patients well again. Their mortal enemy was ECC, short for Evil Crazy Cancer. ECC would fly into hospital rooms and grab patients. He would swing them around until they threw up. With Dr. Batman by his side, Jamal would use a magic baton to chase Evil Crazy Cancer into a corner, where Nurse Robin was waiting with a strong box. Together, they would shrink ECC and push him into the box. Triumphantly, they did a crazy victory dance around the box, singing, "We got you, ECC. You were easy, easy, easy. We got you, ECC. You were easy, easy, easy!"

Jamal felt powerful. He loved pretending to be a superhero who used his powers to make his mother better. He felt like he was saving the day!

Directions

Create a superhero who can save people's lives.

Questions

What will you name your superhero?

_____

_____

How will your superhero save lives?

_____

_____

_____

_____

_____

_____

What would you like to ask your superhero?

_____

_____

_____

_____

_____

For You to Think About

When adults are expressing their sadness about the death of your loved one, they may want you to talk about the person who died. It may be a time when you would prefer to play, and that's okay. You can just say that there are things you'd rather be doing at that moment, and offer to talk at another time.

Sabina and her family had just finished dinner. Mom suggested that they all go to the cemetery the next day. Her grandpa had been buried there last month, and since then, Sabina had been there several times. She didn't feel like going again. She had a play date planned and was looking forward to swimming with her friend. Sabina felt confused, angry, and frustrated. She loved her grandfather but didn't want to go to the cemetery. She didn't know how to tell her mother.

The next day, while her mother was getting ready to go, Sabina talked with her older sister, Claudia. She said that she felt confused and uncomfortable about wanting to go swimming instead of being with her mother at the cemetery. Claudia helped Sabina explain her feelings to their mother. Their mom understood and said, "It's okay to play and live life the way you did before Grandpa died. We each need to find our own time and place to remember Grandpa. Sometimes we can share it with others, and sometimes we can do it alone." She hugged Sabina, saying, "I'll be fine going alone. It's a beautiful day for swimming, and I hope you have a wonderful time."

Directions

Complete the following story.

One day, Jackie went into her parents' bedroom to ask a question. She found her father and mother crying. Her mom said, "Today is a hard day for us. We miss Sheila terribly." Jackie had been busy playing a video game, and she wasn't sure what to say. _____

_____

_____

_____

_____

_____

_____

_____

_____

_____

_____

_____

_____

_____

Questions

Do you like your story? _____

Would you like to change anything?

_____

_____

_____

_____

Has anything like what happened to Jackie ever happened to you? If so, what did you do?

_____

_____

_____

_____

_____

_____

_____

_____

_____

For You to Think About

When people worry, there are many feelings wrapped up in each worry. There are answers to some worries, and some worries just can't be answered. It is important to share your worries and ask questions about them.

We all worry sometimes. Children may worry about what they will wear to school, the grade they will get on a test, if someone will like them, or if they will make the baseball team. After someone they love has died, they may worry about who will take care of them or whether other people they love will die. They may even worry that they are going to die.

When worries keep you from having fun, sleeping, or doing your schoolwork, it is time to let go of them. There are ways to get rid of your worries, like talking with another person, asking questions about them, or writing them down and putting away what you have written. It is important for you to remember that people often worry about things that never happen, and holding on to worries isn't helpful for you.

Guatemalan Worry Dolls

Directions

Worry dolls are small yarn or string dolls that were first made in Guatemala. Each night before children went to sleep, they would tell the dolls their worries. The legend was that during the night these dolls would take away the children's worries. Decorate the worry dolls below. On the line beneath each doll, write one thing you are worried about.

Why Did You Die?

Questions

Describe any worries that started after your loved one died.

_____

_____

_____

_____

Write the name of a grown-up you can talk with about your worries.

_____

What can you do to help your worries go away?

_____

_____

_____

_____

_____

_____

Activity 31   When You Feel Angry

For You to Think About

When someone you love has died, you may feel angry. Anger can make you feel as if you are going to explode, but there are ways to help you manage your anger and feel better.

Mark had an angry look on his face. He yelled at his sister for sitting too near him. He shouted, "I hate you!" and stomped out of the room. A few minutes later, his mother asked if she could come into his bedroom. When he said yes, she sat down to talk with him. Mark said, "I'm feeling so angry today." His mother asked what was making him angry, but he didn't know how to answer. His mom explained that feelings can be hard to figure out. She said that even if Mark didn't know why he felt angry, telling someone about his feelings would help. He could just say, "I feel angry, and I don't know why!" He could squeeze a pillow or exercise or breathe deeply until he felt calmer. He could also think about how being angry made his body feel. Did he feel hot? Tense? Did his stomach or his head hurt?

They sat together for a while, and Mark's mom asked, "Would you like to go for a bike ride together?" He shrugged, but he followed her to the garage and they got out their bikes. After their ride, his mother asked, "How do you feel now?" With a smile, Mark said, "Better!"

Directions

In the space below, draw a volcano erupting. In the lava flow, write the feelings that are erupting from the volcano.

Questions

Write about a time you felt like erupting.

_____

_____

_____

_____

What did you do about that feeling?

_____

_____

_____

_____

What do you think is a good way for you to handle your angry feelings?

_____

_____

_____

_____

For You to Think About

When someone you love dies, some things in your life will change, but many things will stay the same. Thinking about what has stayed the same can help you feel better.

Bonnie always looked up to her sister Morgan. Morgan was three years older, and she had always been part of Bonnie's life. Their parents told stories about Bonnie, as a baby, following her older sister everywhere. They said that whatever Morgan played with, Bonnie wanted to play with. Their younger sister, Haley, also adored Morgan. Morgan was so patient with her sisters and would play with each of them. Bonnie wasn't so patient with Haley, who often got into her toys and broke things. Morgan never minded if her sisters played with her toys. She was much better at sharing than Bonnie was.

Everything seemed to change when Morgan died. Now Haley always wanted to play with Bonnie, and Bonnie didn't know what to do. She was used to being the middle sister and following her older sister's lead. Morgan always had good ideas about what to play, and Bonnie wanted her back. Her mom was still her mom, her dad was still her dad, and Haley was still her little sister. But without Morgan, she felt like she was in a different family.

Some Things Change and Some Remain the Same

Directions

In the columns below, list things in your life that have changed and things that have remained the same since your loved one died.

Things That Have Changed	Things That Have Stayed the Same

Choose one thing from each column and write how it makes you feel.

_____   _____

Why Did You Die?

Questions

How do you feel about the things that have changed in your life?

_____

_____

_____

_____

How do you feel about the things that have stayed the same?

_____

_____

_____

_____

Activity 33   You Will Always Be You

For You to Think About

You may feel like a different person when someone you love has died. It's important for you to remember that, while some things about you may have changed, you are still the same person you were before the death.

Everything in Michael's life seemed to change after his older brother, Shawn, died. Michael used to go to Shawn for advice. Shawn had taught him all about cars and shown him how to play chess. Now Shawn wasn't there to help him with anything, and Michael felt alone.

At school, everyone knew about Shawn's death. When they asked questions about his family, Michael was upset and confused about what to say. His parents were sad all the time, and the family didn't do much together anymore. He felt like everything was different, and he wasn't even sure if he was the same person.

Michael went to his school counselor, Ms. Griffith. As they talked about all the changes that had taken place in his family, Michael cried. He said he was afraid that he would never be the same again. Ms. Griffith said, "I can see there are parts of you that haven't changed. You are still the same kind and sensitive person. You are still good in math and science. You still have the same friends." Michael smiled and felt relieved to hear some of the things that were still the same.

Directions

In the space on the left, draw a picture of yourself before the death of your loved one. In the space on the right, draw another picture of yourself after the death of your loved one.

Questions

What are you doing in each picture?

_____

_____

_____

_____

_____

What title would you give each picture?

_____

_____

_____

_____

_____

Write five things that are still the same about you.

1. _____

2. _____

3. _____

4. _____

5. _____

For You to Think About

You may have a special place where you go to remember your loved one. It may be the cemetery or a place where the two of you spent time together or any place that helps you think. When you go there, you can take something with you, such as flowers or a letter you have written.

Mother's Day was coming up, and Marcie and Matt were feeling very sad. It was the first Mother's Day since their mom had died. They had always had fun deciding what to give her and weren't sure what to do this year.

For as long as they could remember, their mother had loved to watch birds. One year, Marcie and Matt had made a book where she could keep a list of different birds she had seen. Another year, they had each made a collage using pictures of birds from old magazines. They talked about it together and decided to make a bird feeder for their mother's grave. They covered a pinecone with peanut butter and then rolled it in birdseed.

On Mother's Day, their dad took them to their mother's grave, and they carefully placed the feeder there. The next time they visited, all the seed had been eaten. Picturing their mom enjoying the birds helped them feel better.

Activities to Help Children Cope with Grief and Loss

Taking Something to the Place You Remember Your Loved One

Directions

Make a list of things you can think of to take to the place where you remember your loved one. Put a check next to the ones you think you might take.

Questions

Can you make any of the things you listed?

_____

_____

_____

Have you ever taken anything there? If so, what?

_____

_____

_____

_____

_____

Has anyone else ever left anything? What did you think about what they left?

_____

_____

_____

_____

_____

Activity 35

Things You Wish You Had Said

For You to Think About

After someone you love has died, you may think about all the things you wish you had said or done differently. If the person died suddenly, you may not have had time to say good-bye or to say you were sorry about something. Even if you had time, you may have felt uncomfortable saying those things. What is important to remember is that your loved one knew you loved him or her.

Jamie cried to her mother, "I didn't get to say good-bye to Daddy." She was so sad that she would never have the chance to tell him that she had gotten an A on a math test he helped her study for. She wanted to thank him for buying her favorite waffles. She was sorry she had argued with him because he asked her to make the sound lower when she was listening to her new CD. Most of all, she wanted to say, "I love you. You're the best dad!"

Her mom said, "You can tell Daddy these things in your prayers. You can say them when you visit his grave. You can even write them in a letter." Jamie liked the idea of writing a letter. She could imagine her dad reading over her shoulder, like he used to when he helped with her homework. Her mom gave Jamie stationery to write the letter. When she had finished, she felt much better. Jamie put her letter in a special box where she kept things that had belonged to her father.

Directions

Take the time to think of all the things you would like to say to your loved one. Make a copy of the following page, cut out the stationery, and write your letter on it. If you would like, you may decorate the page. When you have finished, fold and seal your letter.

_____

_____

_____

_____

_____

_____

_____

_____

_____

_____

_____

_____

Things You Wish You Had Said

Questions

How did it feel to write this letter?

_____

_____

_____

_____

_____

_____

Do you want to share it with anyone?

_____

Where do you want to keep your letter?

_____

_____

_____

_____

_____

> ## *For You to Think About*
>
> Creating a special place is one way to honor people who have died. Memorials, mausoleums, tombstones, and plaques are all places that we visit to remember these people.

Bryan's class went on a trip to Washington, D.C. Bryan was very impressed by all the monuments, statues, and buildings. He was especially touched by the Vietnam Veterans Memorial, a long, tall, black wall engraved with the names of soldiers who had died in the Vietnam War. People had placed flowers, candles, and other items along the wall to honor their loved ones. Bryan saw people searching for their loved ones' names. Some people were crying, some were praying, and some were sharing stories.

Bryan told his teacher that he wished he could make a memorial for his father, who had died of cancer the year before. Bryan remembered all the medical treatments his father had undergone and how many times he had been in the hospital. Bryan was proud of his father, who had never given up trying to get well. He thought of his dad as a soldier who fought hard against his illness but didn't survive, like the veterans whose names were on the wall. His teacher suggested that he could design a memorial for his father when they returned to school. Bryan was excited about this idea. On the bus ride home, he began planning his design.

Directions

In the space below, design a memorial for your loved one.

Questions

What do you like about the memorial you designed?

_____

_____

_____

_____

Is there anything you dislike?

_____

_____

_____

_____

If people could visit this memorial, how do you think it would make them feel? Why?

_____

_____

_____

_____

Activity 37 Memories Are Important

For You to Think About

You can remember your loved one in your thoughts. Photographs, items that belonged to the person, and other keepsakes can also remind you of them.

Julie's mother had died ten months ago, and Julie missed her very much. One night before she went to sleep, Julie talked with her dad about how sad she felt. She was afraid she wouldn't remember her mom.

The next night after dinner, her father suggested a project for the two of them to work on together. He said, "I bought a scrapbook today. I thought it was time for us to put all our photos together in a memory book." That evening, they went through the photographs and decided which ones they would put in their book. There were photographs of her mother holding Julie as a newborn baby and hugging Julie at her kindergarten graduation. There were pictures of the two of them swimming at the lake and several from Thanksgiving dinners with the whole family. Julie and her dad spent the whole evening looking at the pictures and sharing their memories. The next night they would begin organizing the scrapbook, using different paper, markers, and stickers to decorate the pages.

At breakfast the following morning, Julie told her dad that she realized she would never forget her mom. Her father kissed her and said, "Julie, whenever you want to, we can look at things to help us remember Mom."

Why Did You Die?

Directions

Decorate the frame below. Then place a photograph or draw a picture that shows your favorite memory of you with your loved one.

Questions

How old were you when this event happened? _____

Where were you, and was anyone else with you?

_____

_____

_____

Would you like to go back to this time?

_____

_____

_____

How does this memory make you feel?

_____

_____

_____

_____

_____

_____

Sharing Memories with Others

For You to Think About

Sharing your memories of your loved one with a group of people can be helpful. Some people might have known your loved one, and some people may want to listen to your stories or tell their own.

Melissa's mother wanted her to join a new support group for people who had lost someone they loved. Melissa refused, saying, "I don't want to talk with anybody!" Finally, her mother convinced her to try it. The group was going to meet once a week, and before the first meeting, Melissa was prepared to hate it.

At the beginning of group, everyone said their names and ages and told something about the person in their family who had died. Before that afternoon, Melissa had never told a group of people about her sister's death. It was difficult to do, but Melissa was pleased with herself once she said the words. No one in the group seemed surprised. All the other kids were around her age, and they all had had someone they loved die.

Everyone in the group made a collage to introduce themselves. Melissa was surprised that she was having fun. There were many magazines to choose pictures from, and the group members shared all the art materials. After they completed their collages, the group leader asked each of them to talk about their artwork. Melissa learned a lot about the other members, and it felt like she had already known them for a long time. They all told stories about their loved ones, and everyone had so much to say that the group leader had to remind them to take turns and listen. Even Melissa joined in!

Melissa learned a lot about herself, too. She found out that she wasn't the only kid who had had a family member die, and that other kids had some of the same feelings she did. She realized that she didn't have to hide the fact that her sister had died. The kids in the group weren't afraid to hear her stories; they were actually interested. When her mother took her home that day, she asked, "So, what did you think?" Melissa casually answered, "It was okay." Each week after that, Melissa attended the meeting, but it wasn't until months later that she finally admitted to her mother how much she liked being a part of it.

Directions

Complete this quilt to share what you would like others to know about your loved one. You can use drawing materials, copies of photographs, magazines pictures, or any other materials you choose. The squares can be created alone, or you can work with a family member or friend.

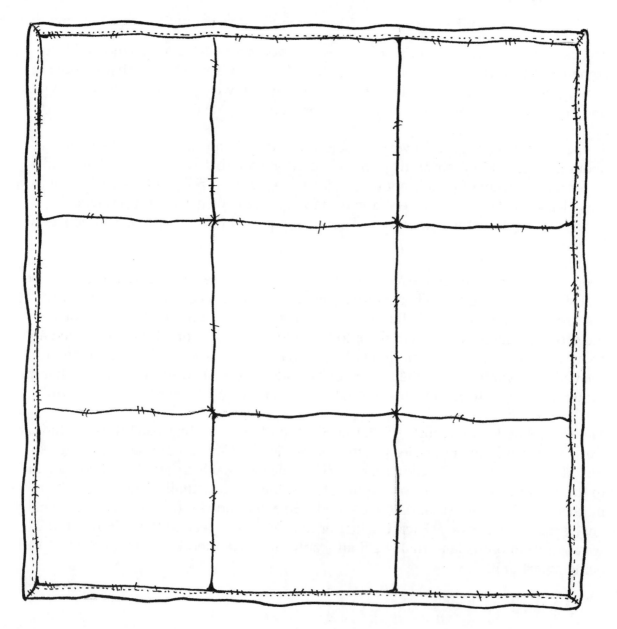

Why Did You Die?

Questions

Did anyone help you with your quilt? If not, was there someone you might have liked to ask?

_____

Is there anything missing from the quilt squares?

_____

_____

_____

_____

Would you like to give this quilt to someone or hang it somewhere?

_____

_____

_____

_____

Activity 39   Life Has Ups and Downs

> ## *For You to Think About*
>
> Life can be like a roller-coaster ride, with ups and downs, with good days, bad days, and in-between days. On bad days, it can help to remember that the next day things can change for the better.

On Saturday morning, Kyle had soccer practice. He worked hard on his skills, and the coach complimented him on his improvement. Kyle was feeling confident and proud. When he walked into his house, his mother had bad news. While Kyle was at practice, his dog had been hit by a car. Kyle's mood went crashing down, down, down.

Theresa's brother was ill and in the hospital. One day during school, she was feeling especially sad and worried. Music was one of Theresa's favorite subjects, but that day she didn't feel like singing. Not wanting to get in trouble with her teacher, she sang along anyway. Before long, Theresa was singing with energy and wasn't thinking about any of her worries. Her mood went rising up, up, up.

Directions

In each car at the top of the roller coaster, write one thing that puts you in a good mood. In each car at the bottom, write one thing that puts you in a bad mood. On the lines below, write what you can do to help change each bad mood into a good mood.

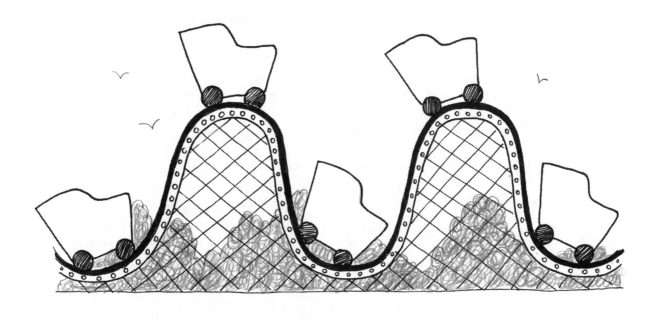

_____   _____   _____

_____   _____   _____

Questions

Write about a time when your mood changed quickly.

_____

_____

_____

_____

_____

_____

_____

_____

What usually helps you when you are feeling down?

_____

_____

_____

_____

_____

_____

_____

Taking Care of Yourself

For You to Think About

You probably know many ways to take care of your body. Eating healthy snacks, brushing your teeth, and getting enough sleep are some ways to meet your body's needs. It's also important to take care of your feelings. When you have uncomfortable feelings, there are things you can do to help yourself feel better.

Hannah loved to exercise. When she swam or danced or even just went for a walk, she felt better for the rest of the day. She felt confident, energetic, and happy. Hannah knew that exercise was an important way to take care of her body.

Sometimes, Hannah felt sad or angry or scared. When that happened, she didn't enjoy doing things, even activities that she usually liked. Her mom said that Hannah could take care of her feelings, just like she took care of her body. Together, she and her mom made a list of ways to help Hannah feel better:

- Write in your journal
- Draw a picture
- Talk with someone about how you feel
- Listen to music
- Cuddle
- Ride your bike
- Watch a favorite movie

The next time Hannah felt sad, she thought about the list she had created with her mom. She took out her crayons and a large piece of paper, and she drew a picture of what was bothering her. As she drew, she felt her sadness going away.

Directions

Make a list of things that you can do to make yourself feel better. On the next page, draw a picture of yourself doing one of the things you listed.

Things I Can Do to Make Myself Feel Better

_____   _____

_____   _____

_____   _____

_____   _____

_____   _____

_____   _____

_____   _____

Questions

Which activities do you do very often?

_____

_____

_____

_____

_____

Which is your favorite activity?

_____

_____

_____

Which one do you think would help you feel better when you are sad?

_____

_____

_____

Erika Leeuwenburgh, LPC, is a licensed professional counselor, board-certified art therapist and child life specialist. In 1987 she established a pediatric psychosocial program for children with the Joseph M. Sanzari Children's Hopital at Hackensack University Medical Center in Hackensack, NJ. This Child Life/Creative Arts Therapy program provides comprehensive psychosocial support services for infants, children and adolescents with art, music, dance/movement, drama therapists and child life specialists. Her clinical work focuses predominantly upon hospitalized, chronically ill, or bereaved children and their parents, and children whose parents are critically ill. She is an assistant visiting professor at Pratt Institute in Brooklyn, NY where she has taught for more than 10 years. She lectures nationally and has published several articles.

Ellen Goldring, LPC, is a board-certified and registered art therapist and certified child life specialist. She is currently a supervisor of Child Life/Creative Arts Therapy Services at Joseph M. Sanzari Children's Hopital at Hackensack University Medical Center in Hackensack, NJ. She offers therapy for the children of adults with life-threatening illnesses and for medically ill patients and siblings, and has developed children's bereavement programming.

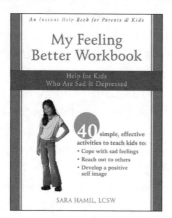

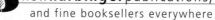